introduction to
TWENTIETH
CENTURY
DESIGN
from the collection of
THE MUSEUM OF MODERN ART
new york

by arthur drexler and greta daniel

distributed by Doubleday & Company, Inc., Garden City, New York

CONTENTS

PREFACE

When the Museum was founded in 1929 it was proposed by Alfred H. Barr, Jr., its first director, that standards be defined and history written for architecture and design just as for painting and sculpture. Still the only institution to include a curatorial department devoted to architecture and design, the Museum since 1932 has exhibited and collected material relevant to these two arts, as well as graphic design (posters and typography).

Buildings, of course, can be "collected" only through models and photographs of little intrinsic value, but there have been many collections of objects. Traditionally such material has been called "decorative arts." The Museum's Collection is concerned primarily with mass-produced useful objects made to serve a specific purpose, and so the term design, or industrial design, has been used instead.

The Design Collection now comprises some 850 examples, representing all the arts of manufacture and classified within the following categories: household furnishings and office equipment; tableware; tools; furniture; and textiles. In size and diversity they range from such mass-produced artifacts as pillboxes, typewriters and radios to chairs and tables. There are handmade objects by individual craftsmen, and even such semi-architectural productions as the entrance arch to a Paris Métro station.

Material for the Design Collection is assembled by the Department's staff. Their recommendations are presented through the Director of the Museum Collections to a committee comprised principally of trustees. This committee must formally approve design acquisitions (just as it does painting and sculpture) before they can be added to the Museum Collections. In addition the Department maintains a separate study collection for supplementary material of marginal interest.

Small objects are stored on the Museum's premises. Furniture requires ample storage space outside the Museum, but certain very large objects, such as automobiles, although they have been exhibited are not collected because they are too inconvenient to store.

Two criteria apply in the selection of objects: *quality* and *historical significance*.

An object is chosen for its quality because it is thought to achieve, or to have originated, those formal ideals of beauty which have become the major stylistic concepts of our time.

Significance is a more flexible evaluation. It applies to objects not necessarily works of art but which nevertheless have contributed importantly to the development of design.

Probably it is impossible, and perhaps even undesirable, to apply each of these definitions with perfect consistency. For example, "the major stylistic concepts of our time" might be interpreted to include many objects in which inane decoration and clumsy shapes substitute for balance of proportions and fitness for purpose, normally considered basic to good design. But the Department's definition of quality excludes bizarre or merely unsuccessful styles, no matter how numerous their examples may be. The Collection as yet includes no television sets, no refrigerators, no telephones, and only a relatively few mechanical appliances—not because such objects are intrinsically unworthy, but because too often their design is determined by commercial factors irrelevant, or even harmful, to aesthetic quality. Even such sincere but unfortunate manifestations as "modernistic" furniture which, in the 1920s, imitated the stepped contours of skyscrapers, are not eligible for inclusion. Finally, it should be noted that a good many objects in the Collection, representing a generally high standard of achievement, could be replaced by others just as fine.

Objects are acquired through gifts from manufacturers, designers and interested private persons, and through purchase funds. Substantial additions to the Collection have been made by gifts from Edgar Kaufmann, Jr. and Philip Johnson. Purchase funds have been most notably augmented by generous gifts from Mrs. Phyllis Lambert, the Lambert Fund having in fact made possible the Department's recent acquisition of much Art Nouveau, Bauhaus and current European material.

Exhibitions at the Museum have afforded many opportunities to assemble important groups of objects. Indeed the Design Collection may be said to have begun with the Machine Art exhibition organized in 1934 by Philip Johnson, the Department's first director. Some 100 objects from the exhibition provided the nucleus of a Collection intended from the beginning to document design characteristics peculiar to the twentieth century. The standards defined at that time by Philip Johnson and Alfred H. Barr, Jr. gave the Collection its basic character. Under the Department's present director, and with the administration of Greta Daniel, Associate Curator of Design, it has been expanded along the lines first proposed by its founders.

John MacAndrew, Curator of what was then called the Department of Architecture and Industrial Art from 1937 to 1940, and Eliot Noyes, Director of a separate Department of Industrial Design from 1940 to 1945, made valuable additions to the Collection through exhibitions and competitions. Notable among these was a series initiated by John MacAndrew called "Useful Objects." Successive exhibitions acquainted the public with inexpensive good design, the price range eventually being broadened so that furniture and mechanical appliances could also be shown. Eliot Noyes' competition in 1940, called "Organic Design in Home Furnishings," led to the manufacture of prize-winning designs. Chairs by Charles Eames and Eero Saarinen now in the Collection derive from this project.

After this series perhaps the most important group of exhibitions, both as a public service and as a potential source of Collection material, was the program called "Good Design." Directed by Edgar Kaufmann, Jr., from 1950 to 1955 the "Good Design" exhibitions sought to influence the wholesale buyers who determine what furnishings will appear in stores throughout the country; to convince manufacturers of the potentially large market for well designed objects; and to encourage designers by the example of good work and the possibility of wide recognition. In collaboration with the Merchandise Mart in Chicago, the Museum presented each year (bi-annually in Chicago) work produced in the United States and abroad during the one year period under review. Examples were acquired for the Collection from each exhibition.

There has never been sufficient gallery space to keep even a small part of the Design Collection permanently on view. This fact is of considerable importance, particularly in relation to the Museum's program of design exhibitions. For example, with the Collection chronically hidden in storerooms the public had no opportunity to measure each year's "Good Design" selections against the best work in a Collection covering a period of roughly 65 years.

The effort to assist designers, manufacturers and the public in improving standards of design continues to be a major part of the Museum's program. In the winter of 1958-59, the Museum exhibited for the first time a major part of the Design Collection—an appropriate step in clarifying the origin and development of ideas which have determined the appearance of artifacts in the twentieth century. And, like painting and sculpture, design offers great pleasure. A thousand years from now the Design Collection, we may hope, will provide an invaluable record of what seemed to be some of the most beautiful artifacts of our time. Many of them do indeed rival in beauty and significance the best that survives from previous civilizations.

But there are historical gaps in this Collection. Some of them are due to the restricted production of the artists themselves. Thus the extraordinarily influential Dutch Stijl architects and designers executed relatively little work either in architecture or design, and the Collection includes exactly four Stijl objects, all of them by Gerrit Rietveld. Work by members of the Bauhaus school, though much more numerous, remains difficult to assemble. The Collection still lacks certain examples relevant to the part played by this movement in establishing internationally a style of design related to machine production. Although the Art Nouveau material includes particularly interesting groups of Guimard furniture and Tiffany glass, there is not yet one example of the furniture or other objects designed by Henry van de Velde.

A more concerted effort ought to be made to appraise and collect work from Russia and the Central European nations as well as from Latin America. China, India and other Asian countries will soon be contributing to the aesthetics of industrialized civilization; Japan already has.

It is hoped that these gaps will be filled. Toward this end the Department continues to welcome, and indeed requires, assistance from individual collectors and patrons as well as from the manufacturers and designers of work in current production.   —A.D.

INTRODUCTION

If asked to decide what it is that makes an object look "modern," most people would probably think first of "simplicity." That at least is a word they might choose if a certain kind of simplicity elicits their approval. If it does not, they might instead think of the words "bare" and "cold." And, if they have thought about the subject at all, they are quite likely to remember the word "functional."

Some contemporary objects, like pots and pans, are modifications of basic designs as old as civilization. Others, like telephones and radios, are without precedent and the shapes they are given must be invented. In both cases the shapes that most readily suggest the twentieth century are usually geometric, precisely finished, smooth, and without the elaboration and variety of detail we associate with the craftsman's handiwork.

The number and kind of mechanical objects on which our lives now depend have changed our habits. We dress, walk, and even sit differently; we live in smaller rooms, have fewer servants, and spend less time in our homes. For all these reasons we have come to expect that the objects with which we surround ourselves will not only be agreeable to look at but will also contribute actively to our comfort. We require that objects do something and that they do it well. But the idea that the appearance of any object (other than a tool) should be determined primarily by its function is relatively new, as is the related idea that if only an object be truly functional, its shape *must* be beautiful.

The doctrine of functionalism has swept away much Victorian clutter and in some ways has greatly simplified our lives. This is all the more remarkable when one considers that there are probably no two people who can agree on what constitutes a satisfactory functional performance for even so simple an object as a chair. No two people have quite the same shape. Should the conscientious designer construct a chair for what he takes to be the general shape most people have? Or should he rather allow for the widest possible variety of human shapes? Should he assume that the same chair will be used for reading, eating, conversing, and slouching, or should he assume that each of these performances merits a chair unto itself? It is not possible to define function as if it were an attribute of an object itself, when in reality it is a complex of relationships between habits and accidents of use, techniques of fabrication, and symbolic meanings.

Functionalism has had its greatest influence in and through architecture. Every one of the major innovations of modern furniture design has been the work of an architect: Ludwig Mies van der Rohe, Le Corbusier, Alvar Aalto, Marcel Breuer, Charles Eames. Because little appropriate furniture existed for their buildings, modern architects were often forced to design not only new furniture but also new hardware and equipment. The training of designers to understand the requirements of machine production, and then to design all kinds of artifacts in a style that would relate to both the manner in which they were made and to the kind of life in which they would be used, was done most effectively at the Bauhaus school in Germany from 1919 to 1933. The faculty of this institution included painters and sculptors as well as architects and designers, and many members were competent in several arts.

For a number of reasons, among them the fact that machines themselves were largely composed of geometric, precisely finished shapes, Bauhaus designers assumed that objects made by machines must necessarily exhibit the same characteristics. But most of the products of the Bauhaus workshops were made by hand. When these designs were acquired by industry for mass production, it was often necessary to make certain modifications for the sake of economy or to overcome technical difficulties. Unfortunately such adjustments usually deprived a design of just that kind of detail that had given the hand-made prototype its machine-made look.

The preoccupation with the "look" of being machine-made was in fact so basic to much early modern design that it affected painters and sculptors as well as craftsmen. It also established our notion of what is a suitable aesthetic expression of machine techniques. Still more importantly, it revealed a nervous hostility towards mechanization. The prevailing image of the modern world (and the world of tomorrow) in the 'twenties and 'thirties was that of a super-metropolis, itself like a machine, sinister, and disquietingly indifferent to variations in human behavior. In exchange for wealth the machine seemed to impose internal poverty. And yet a return to pre-industrial forms of social organization was a practical impossibility, and contrary to the rational thought that developed machines to begin with.

One result of this concern for the ethics of machine production was a desire to devaluate objects as works of art. Now that society could produce as much as it wanted, the individual artifact was no longer an accurate index of wealth or an appropriate vehicle for nonmaterial values. Exuberance for its own sake, baroque declamation, seemed merely bad taste. Underlying the geometric and somewhat aggressive functional style were theories of aesthetics contributed by artists almost entirely indifferent to their practical implications; but a sense of urgency, of a moral imperative, adapted these theories to a purpose of both practical and ethical significance. Functionalism's moral imperative made it the artist's responsibility to temper creation with propriety, and it also encouraged him to participate in programs of social and economic reform.

Most great designers and architects have sustained quite personal interpretations of functionalism, and have not in practice allowed their favorite aesthetic preconceptions to be entirely overruled by a moral judgment. Others have sometimes chosen to define functionalism in psychological as well as mechanistic terms, so that its program would include the satisfaction of a wide variety of emotional needs. In practice this interpretation has most often been used to justify the pseudo-traditional pastiche, admired for its "warmth" and "charm."

By the middle of the twentieth century the idea of function has come to be considered in a somewhat broader way. It no longer refers only to the use an object serves. Now it may also be understood to include the manner in which objects are *manufactured, distributed,* and *maintained.* During the last two decades problems of distribution and maintenance in particular have increased, and nowhere more than in the United States. Characteristic problems of the American economy have to do not with the production of wealth but with its use; not with producing enough to go around but with persuading people to use more than they think they need; not with learning to conserve wealth but with persuading people to throw away what their grandfathers would have repaired.

The expense of preparing machinery for mass production involves the manufacturer in a great gamble. To minimize this risk he makes what he believes the public requires. Any departure from what most people are presumed to want must necessarily reduce the potential number of customers. Techniques of mass production have ensured that the manufacture of an object in enormous quantities is possible only for an equally enormous group of people — who must all want the same object.

Excellence is normally considered to describe quality rather than quantity. What is excellent is also usually rare. It follows that a manufacturer who has made a great investment in machinery will not always undertake to produce objects for the small group of people habitually concerned with excellence. But since no one likes to think of himself as being concerned exclusively with mediocrity, our notions of what constitutes excellence have undergone such modifications as will allow millions of people to subscribe to them.

This conversion of standards, conducted by the advertising industry, assumes among other things that the manufacturer and his research experts really are able to determine what the public thinks it wants. There are many reasons for believing that they are not in fact able to do so. They can, however, encourage the public to choose products on the strength of irrelevant associations (economic

status, authority, etc.). The appetites such a program stimulates can never be satisfied by the products themselves; advertising, like Cleopatra, "makes hungry where she most satisfies."

Nevertheless, there are of course innumerable objects excellent both in performance and appearance, and there is still meaningful variety. But except in the larger American cities the only collections of industrial design seen by the public are those on the display counters of local stores. The individuals who each year choose the merchandise stores will offer their customers are thus in a position of peculiar responsibility. They will not lightly undertake to propose standards different from those they believe their customers prefer, but if they avoid what is excellent or exceptional they further discourage its production. In Germany the Braun company, a manufacturer of radios and kitchen equipment, uses the money normally invested in advertising for the education of store personnel, who are taken at the company's expense to schools where they are taught some of the principles which make for excellence of design. In the United States, museums and some publications attempt a similar service for the general public. Many Japanese department stores consider it both their responsibility and prerogative to exhibit objects drawn from great private and public collections, including those of the Imperial Household and the national museums, and the standards of selection are comparable with those applied by museums in this country. But to most American stores such a program would seem evangelical, or antipathetic to profit.

Perhaps the most significant changes in distribution our stores have made in recent years are in the physical organization of the store itself and in the extension of credit. The suburban shopping centers promise to become great supply depots around which houses, schools, and local government offices might cluster as once they did around the village church. Credit systems encourage the acquisition of objects many families might otherwise have managed happily without, and credit makes it appropriate to replace these objects with new ones ever more rapidly.

Few families in the United States today think of the furnishings they buy, much less their houses, as potential heirlooms for their children. Houses as well as furnishings are now attractive properties according to the ease with which they may be disposed of, not retained. This has contributed to the uniformity of much residential architecture at least as importantly as have other economic factors. As equipment becomes more complicated to use and expensive to maintain, it is often cheaper to throw it away than to repair it. (No one has yet given national distribution in the United States to an invisible product called *service*.)

Since we wish to be able to transfer our possessions to others without difficulty, and tend to avoid maintenance, we are beginning to welcome objects that are completely expendable. The degree of expendability varies, ranging from the automobile, with its time limit on durability and monetary value, to such conveniences as cheap kitchen artifacts consumed in their first use.

All these tendencies have been readily accepted by the public and energetically advanced by manufacturers. Such questioning as they have undergone has been concerned not with their desirability but with how they may be made more effective. Yet there is one aspect of industrialization that is almost never questioned. Industrialization and technology represent man's refusal to accept poverty and hardship as if they were irremediable facts of nature. Instead, we now accept machinery itself as if it were a fact of nature, given to us with its present limitations for all time. We do allow ourselves the possibility of machines able to dispense with direct control by human beings; no one can seriously argue against the fact that what is called automation will free us from tasks for which we are ill-suited, and that ultimately we shall derive a profound advantage from what Norbert Wiener has described as the human use

of human beings. Characteristically, we are not much surprised that the new kind of machinery should be just as inflexible as the old, in that the only way it can justify its initial cost is to produce the same object in enormous quantities.

Instead of coping with uncontrolled productivity by forcing consumption, often through methods plainly anti-social, we might just as well put our energy into inventing systems capable of limited and alternating cycles of production. We might now attempt to diversify the capacities of machines. Rather than make a million models of the same automobile, for example, machine systems might be designed so that production could be divided economically and at a moment's notice among entirely different kinds of automobiles. Different, of course, refers to fundamental differences and not to arbitrary modifications stuck on like tail fins.

Technical problems involved in modifying the nature of machinery are not the chief obstacle to such an enterprise. A more important obstacle is the confusion between ends and means. Technology often seems to be teaching us that the process by which things are made is more important than the things themselves. If we were to act accordingly, the designer's creative effort might shift away from static, absolute values (of which the geometric machine art "purity" of the early twentieth century is an example) towards the design of the process — the machines themselves.

Our word technology is derived from the Greek word for art: *techne*. We have separated these two concepts so thoroughly that it is now difficult to imagine a reconciliation. But it is no longer possible to view either art or technology as if they were separate events. Technology is an expression of the creative mind. If we are ever to apply qualitative values to its manifestations, we must also be prepared to alter our notions about quality, about art, and about the creative process.

— ARTHUR DREXLER

NEW TECHNIQUES:
THONET BENTWOOD FURNITURE

In 1856 the German Michael Thonet perfected a process by which solid lengths of beechwood could be steamed and bent to form long curved rods. Before the development of this technique, the design of most furniture depended on more or less sculptural joints for the intersections of separate pieces of wood. Bentwood made it possible to eliminate intricate hand-carved joints and contours, and led to the first mass production of standardized furniture. The Austrian firm of Gebrüder Thonet circulated catalogues illustrating their products, and thousands of bentwood chairs were sold throughout the world.

One piece of bentwood could be made to form both the rear legs and backrest of a chair, as in the famous "Vienna" café model still in production (2). The increased continuity of design produced by this simplification also allowed the supporting elements of a chair to be given decorative value merely by extending them in ornamental curves. An example is the flamboyantly elegant rocker (3). The lightness of the bentwood frames is emphasized by seat and back panels of semi-transparent woven cane.

A few Thonet designs achieved a simplification that has made them particularly appealing to twentieth century designers. The most notable is the wood armchair (1) selected by Le Corbusier in the 1920s for use in buildings he had designed because, in his words, "We believe that this chair, whose millions of representatives are used on the continent and in the two Americas, possesses nobility."

1

2

GEBRUDER THONET. Austria. Company designs.

1 ARMCHAIR. c. 1870. Bent beechwood. 31″ h.
Gift of Thonet Industries, Inc. 28.49.

2 "VIENNA" CAFÉ CHAIR. 1876. Bent beechwood.
33½″ h.
Purchase. 444.56.

3 ROCKING CHAIR. 1860. Bent beechwood; cane.
37½″ h.
Gift of Café Nicholson. 459.51.

3

4

4 VASE. c.1900. Carved translucent pink and blue
glass. 16″ h.
EMILE GALLÉ. French. 1846-1904.
Mfr.: Emile Gallé, Nancy, France.
Purchase. 463.56.
Markings: Emile Gallé (facsimile signature).

HECTOR GUIMARD. French. 1867-1942.

5 UMBRELLA STAND. c.1902. Bronze. 32¾″ h.
SIDE CHAIR. c.1912. Cherry; plush upholstery.
43½″ h.
DESK CHAIR. c.1905. Walnut; leather. 32¼″ h.
Gifts of Mme. Hector Guimard. 314.49; 312.49;
311.49.
Designed for the architect's own house at 122
Rue Mozart, Paris.

5

ART NOUVEAU

Art Nouveau flourished from approximately
1893 to 1910. It was the first movement in the
arts to break with the custom — prevalent in
the nineteenth century — of imitating past
styles.

Like the painting of Van Gogh, Gauguin
and Lautrec, Art Nouveau was influenced by
the curvilinear patterns of Japanese prints
at that time popular in Europe and America.
The sinuous whiplash curve became Art Nouveau's typical contour, embracing everything
from poster design to architecture with forms
often reminiscent of plants and flowers.

In furniture designed by the French architect Hector Guimard various elements were
joined so that they appeared to flow into each
other (5). Usually his designs were symmetri-
cal but in some larger pieces, and often in the
applied decoration, he broke with tradition by
composing asymmetrically. The large desk designed for his own use not only employs what
are now called free-form shapes, but also
anticipates today's practice of grouping separate storage elements in a convenient L plan
(10). Guimard's famous entrance arch for the
Paris subway system suggests giant stalks,
each one drooping under the weight of what
seems to be a swollen tropical flower—actually an amber glass lighting fixture (6).

In the United States Louis Comfort Tiffany
perfected, in the 1880s, a process for making
iridescent glass, to which he gave the name
"favrile." It glowed with the kind of color
caused by chemical changes in glass objects
that have long been buried in the earth, like

those found in Roman and Persian excava-
tions. The decoration of Tiffany's vases often
recalls Japanese sources (27). Fascinated by
organic forms, Tiffany utilized the fluidity of
glass to suggest the growth and movement of
flowers (29, 30).

The Germans tended to regard Art Nouveau's break with tradition as an opportunity
to simplify design. Their interest also cen-
tered on new shapes rather than decoration.
Both Richard Riemerschmid and Peter Behrens were commissioned by industry to design
objects for mass production and may perhaps
be considered the first professional industrial designers in today's sense of the term
(15, 16).

Related in spirit to the German movement
was the work of the Scottish architect Charles
Rennie Mackintosh. Like his architecture, his
furniture is often straight-lined and em-
phatically linear, and makes much decorative
use of structural elements (18). For this reason in particular his work is both marginal to
the main direction of Art Nouveau and closer
to the revolution in architecture and design of
the 1920s.

The forms of Art Nouveau did not derive
from structural necessity but were instead
decorative ideas imposed on a variety of materials. The style was notably successful in
objects that are intrinsically decorative or
otherwise eligible for treatment as fantasies.
Although Art Nouveau was short-lived, under
its impetus designers experienced a stimulat-
ing freedom from tradition.

HECTOR GUIMARD. French. 1867-1942.

6   ENTRANCE GATE TO PARIS SUBWAY STATION (MET-
    ROPOLITAIN). c.1900. Cast iron painted green;
    amber glass fixtures. 15′ high, 21′ wide.
    Gift of Régie Autonome des Transports Pari-
    siens. 177.58.
7   DETAIL OF LIGHT FIXTURE.

6

7

HECTOR GUIMARD. French. 1867-1942.

8 SIDE TABLE. c.1908. Pear wood. 43½″ h.

9 DETAIL OF SIDE TABLE.

10 DESK. c.1903. African and olive ash. 28¾″ h.
101″ w.
Gifts of Mme. Hector Guimard. 313.49; 310.49.
Designed for the architect's own house at 122
Rue Mozart, Paris.

8   9

10

11

11 GROUP OF VASES. c.1900. Hand-painted glass.
Des. and Mfr.: DAUM FRÈRES, Nancy, France.
Phyllis B. Lambert Fund. 168.58-174.58.

Daum Frères adapted Gallé's use of modified Renaissance shapes decorated with plant motifs. These vases, however, anticipate later design tendencies by replacing applied decoration with texture.

12 INKSTAND. c.1900. Bronze. 2″ h., c. 8¾″ w.
Designer, manufacturer unknown. French (?).
Phyllis B. Lambert Fund. 104.57.

13 INKSTAND. c.1911. Pewter; blue-green enamel.
3⅜″ h.
Mfr.: Liberty & Co., England. Company
design (?).
Purchase. 105.57.

13

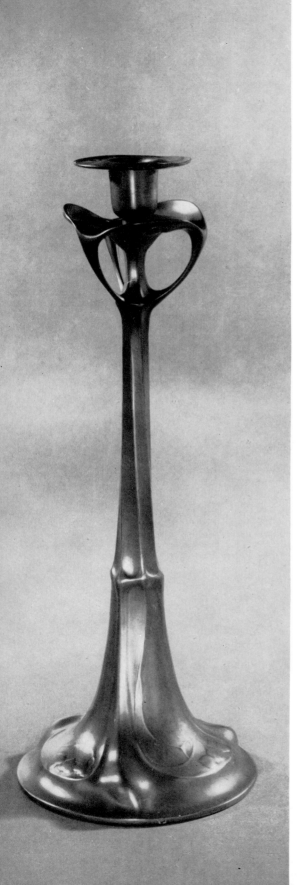

14 CANDLEHOLDER. c.1900. Pewter. 16½″ h.
Mfr.: J. P. Kayser Sohn, Germany. Company design.
Purchase. 490.56.

15 PITCHER. c.1901. Pewter. 4⅛″ h.
PETER BEHRENS. German. 1868-1940.
Mfr.: Gerhardi & Co., Germany.
Phyllis B. Lambert Fund. 166.58.

Designed for the first exhibition of the Mathildenhöhe artists colony, Darmstadt, in 1901.

16 ARMCHAIR. 1899. Mahogany; leather. 31½″ h.
RICHARD RIEMERSCHMID. German. 1868-1957.
Mfr.: Dunbar Furniture Corp. of Indiana, U.S.A.
Gift of the the manufacturer. 125.52.

Contemporary version by agreement between manufacturer and the late Richard Riemerschmid. Original chair designed by Riemerschmid for his music room in the 1899 Exposition in Dresden.

17 JEWEL BOX. c.1900. Silver; mother-of-pearl; turquoise; enamel. 11¼″ x 6″ x 3¼″.
CHARLES KNOX. English. (Executed by William Craythorne.)
Mfr.: Liberty & Co., England.
Gift of the family of Mrs. John D. Rockefeller, Jr. 327.49.

14   15

16

17

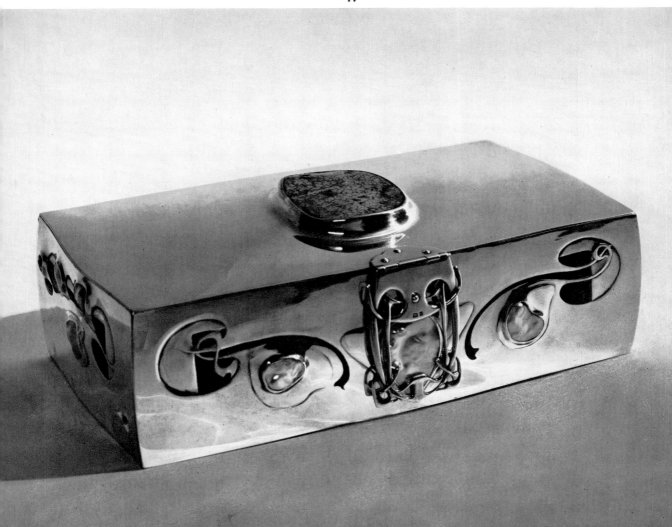

18

19

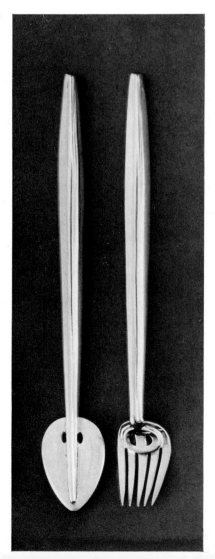

CHARLES RENNIE MACKINTOSH. Scottish. 1868-1928.

18 SIDE CHAIR. 1900. Oak; black silk. 54″ h.
Gift of the Glasgow School of Art. 155.58.
Designed for Mackintosh's own Mains Street apartment in Glasgow.

19 FISH KNIFE AND FORK. c.1900. Silver-plated nickel. 9″ l.
Gift of the University of Glasgow. 214.57.
Designed for either himself or William Davidson, whose house "Windyhill" at Kilmacolm, Mackintosh designed in 1900. From the Davidson Bequest to the University of Glasgow.

LOUIS HENRY SULLIVAN. American. 1865-1924.

20 SPANDREL. c.1898. Cast iron, painted grey. 50″ x 74⅞″.
(Modeled by Kristian Schneider from drawings by Sullivan).
Gift of Dubin & Dubin, Architects, Chicago. 442.56.
Corner panel of decorative frieze from the façade of the Gage Building, Chicago (1898-99). Façade by Sullivan for building by Holabird & Roche.

FRANK LLOYD WRIGHT. American, 1869-1959.

21 OFFICE ARMCHAIR on swivel base. 1904. Painted metal; oak. 37½″ h.
Gift of Edgar Kaufmann, Jr. 185.48.
Designed for the 1904 Larkin Co. office building in Buffalo, New York, the first to be completely furnished with metal office furniture.

22 ARMCHAIR. 1904. Pine; plush upholstery. 32¼″ h.
Gift of Frank Lloyd Wright. 203.47.

20

21

22

24

LOUIS C. TIFFANY. American. 1848-1933.
Mfr.: Tiffany Studios, U.S.A.

23 VASE. c.1900. Favrile glass. 10½" h.
Phyllis B. Lambert Fund. 210.57.
Markings: Louis C. Tiffany 04536

24 VASE. c.1900. Favrile glass. 4⅝" h.
Edgar Kaufmann, Jr. Fund. 192.47.
Markings: L. C. Tiffany Favrile 7265 J
From the Tiffany Foundation Sale, 1946.

25 PURSE. c.1900. Sterling silver; sapphires; baroque pearls; water seal leather. 3" x 4½".
Designer and manufacturer unknown. American (?). Phyllis B. Lambert Fund 213.57.

26 VASE. 1901. Green glazed pottery, pierced.
7½" h.
Mfr.: Rookwood Pottery, U.S.A.,
John D. Wareham, artist.
Phyllis B. Lambert Fund. 112.57.

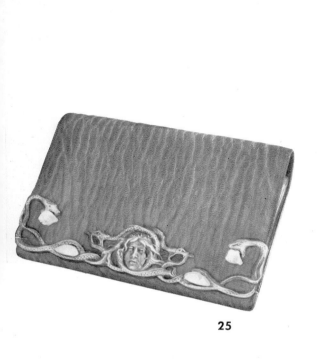

25

26

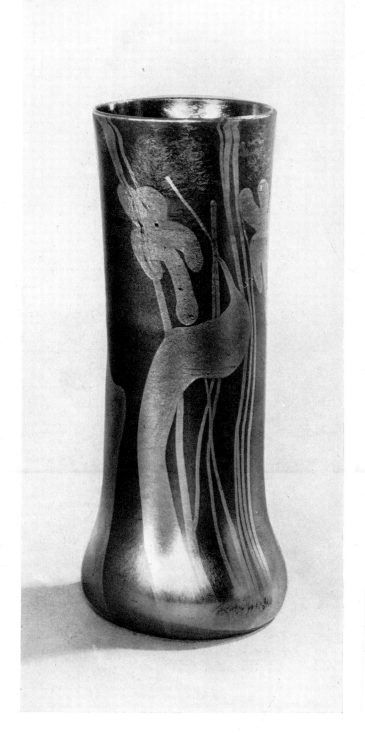

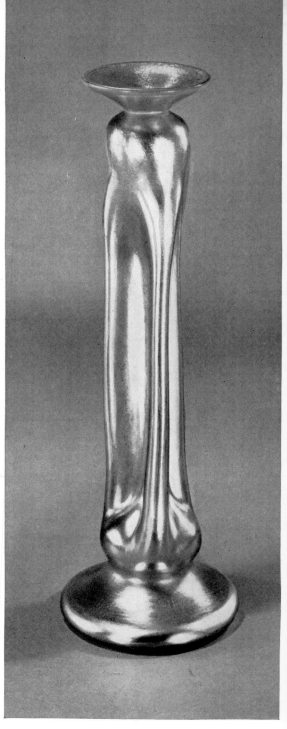

27 VASE. c.1900. Favrile glass. 13¼″ h.
LOUIS C. TIFFANY. American. 1848-1933.
Mfr.: Tiffany Studios, U.S.A.
Edgar Kaufman, Jr. Fund. 232.53.
Markings: Louis C. Tiffany o7501

28 VASE (Candlestick?). c.1900. Favrile glass.
18″ h.
LOUIS C. TIFFANY. American. 1848-1933.
Mfr.: Tiffany Studios, U.S.A.
Phyllis B. Lambert Fund. 93.57.
Markings: L.C.T. Y 7939

29 VASE. c.1900. Favrile glass. 16⅛″ h.
LOUIS C. TIFFANY. American. 1848-1933.
Mfr.: Tiffany Studios, U.S.A.
Phyllis B. Lambert Fund. 99.57.
Markings: L.C.T. W9993 and original label.

30 VASE. c.1900. Favrile glass; silver-plated
bronze. 15⅞″ h.
LOUIS C. TIFFANY. American. 1848-1933.
Mfr.: Tiffany Studios, U.S.A.
Phyllis B. Lambert Fund. 175.58.
Markings: 1795 (glass top). Tiffany Studios,
New York 25695 (base, stamped).

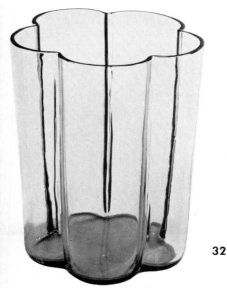

32

CLASSICAL FORM RESTATED

Certain pure classical shapes retained their prestige even after Art Nouveau had broken with tradition. Notable examples are the cups originally designed in 1768 by Josiah Wedgwood (31). These designs are of a classically pure perfection that has continued to satisfy twentieth century judgment.

Josef Hoffmann, foremost among the proponents of Art Nouveau in Austria, the Viennese *Sezession*, at times was also greatly influenced by classical forms. His glass vase (32) is a classical shape stripped of ornament, and his exquisitely fragile tulip-shaped wine glasses (33), possibly the most beautiful of their kind, are serene abstractions of plant forms without extraneous detail. Their effect depends on the impeccable joining of base, stem and bowl, and the precision and clarity with which their contours are defined.

In America at the turn of the century, Frank Lloyd Wright was developing the open plan and horizontal massing of his "prairie house," simplifying or eliminating decoration and preserving the qualities inherent in natural materials. Like Louis Sullivan, Wright emphasized the inter-relation of form and function.

Other architects and designers, attacking Art Nouveau, perceived in the machine rather than in nature a potential unifier of the arts. The Viennese architect Otto Wagner declared in 1894 that "All modern forms must be in harmony with ... the new requirements of our time," and that a future style would emphasize "horizontal lines ... great simplicity and an energetic exhibition of construction and materials."

Adolf Loos, another Viennese architect, maintained that "the lower the standard of the people, the more lavish are its ornaments. To find beauty in form instead of finding it in ornament is the goal toward which humanity is aspiring." Loos regarded engineers as the Hellenes of our culture, relating the geometric forms of classical Greek art to the machine.

31 DEMITASSE AND SAUCER. 1768. Mat-black Basalt ware. 2¼" h.
JOSIAH WEDGWOOD. English. 1730-1795.
Mfr.: Josiah Wedgwood & Sons, Inc., England.
Gift of Josiah Wedgwood & Sons, Inc. of America. 220.54.
From a complete coffee service produced currently from original 18th century molds.

32 VASE. c.1920. Clear green glass. 6" h.
JOSEF HOFFMANN. Austrian. 1870-1956.
Mfr.: J. & L. Lobmeyr, Austria.
Gift of Joseph Binder. 108.48.

33 WINE and CHAMPAGNE GOBLETS. 1920. Clear crystal. 7⅛" h. and 6⅜" h.
JOSEF HOFFMANN. Austrian. 1870-1956.
Mfr.: J. & L. Lobmeyr, Austria.
Gift of A. J. van Dugteren & Son, Inc. 106.48.
CHAMPAGNE GOBLET. 1924. Gold lustre crystal. 10¼" h.
OSWALD HAERDTL. Austrian.
Mfr. and donor as above. 472.56.

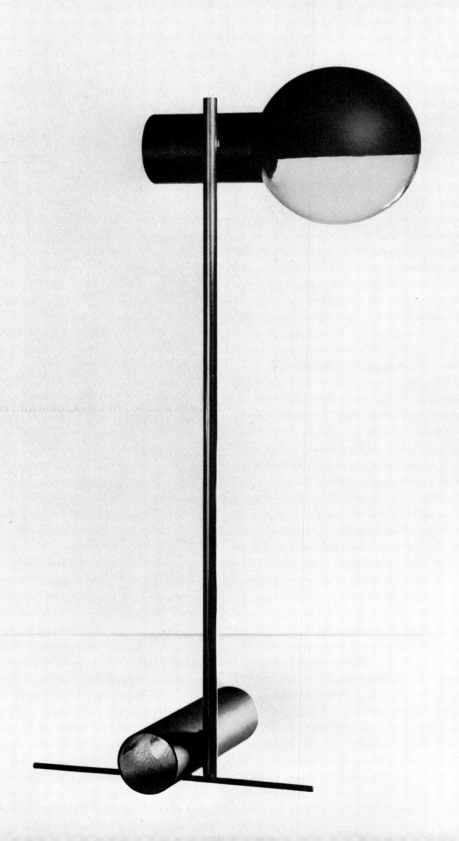

DE STIJL

Initiated by Dutch painters during World War I, de Stijl existed as an organized movement from 1917 to 1928. Its best-known exponents were the painter Piet Mondrian, the painter-architect-writer Theo van Doesburg, the architect Gerrit Rietveld, and the sculptor Georges Vantongerloo.

Like Art Nouveau, de Stijl developed unifying concepts affecting all the arts. But while the richly curvilinear Art Nouveau was dependent on organic forms, de Stijl dispensed with recognizable subject matter. It reduced the elements of composition to independent rectangles and circles; replaced traditional symmetry with freely asymmetrical balance; and used clear, flat primary colors.

Commissioned to design furniture for a house by the Dutch architect Robert van 't Hoff, Gerrit Rietveld complied with the client's request that he model his work on furniture by Frank Lloyd Wright (page 23). One result, his wood armchair of 1917, achieves an appearance of relative weightlessness by the separation of supporting and supported parts, which are painted in black, blue and red (36). Horizontal elements do not rest directly on their vertical supports but are made to bypass each other. The actual manner of physical connection is obscured and the pieces seem to adhere by magnetism. The same principle is used with delicate precision to join a greater variety of shapes in Rietveld's small table lamp (34), the functional aspects of which were of little interest to the designer.

Although Stijl architects actually executed very few buildings, the movement had great influence through its artists and writers. From 1917 to 1932 the group published a magazine which circulated throughout Europe. Van Doesburg himself traveled widely and lectured at the Bauhaus, where Stijl principles decisively influenced subsequent work. Indeed, the theories advanced by Stijl artists still provide the basic formal aesthetic of much modern design and most modern architecture.

34 TABLE LAMP. 1924. Chrome-plated and painted metal; glass. 15″ h.
GERRIT RIETVELD. Dutch, born 1888.
Gift of the designer. 488.53.
This is a replica of the original 1924 design, made by Rietveld in 1953 for the Museum of Modern Art Design Collection.

35 COLOR CONSTRUCTION (Project for a private house). 1922. Gouache on paper. 22½" sq.
THEO VAN DOESBURG. Dutch. 1883-1931; and
CORNELIS VAN EESTEREN. Dutch, born 1897.
Edgar Kaufmann, Jr. Fund. 149.47.

36 ARMCHAIR. 1917. Painted wood. 34½" h.
GERRIT RIETVELD. Dutch, born 1888.
Gift of Philip Johnson. 487.53.

37

37 TEAPOT. 1924. Nickel silver; ebony. 3⅝" h.
MARIANNE BRANDT. German, born 1893.
Manufactured at Bauhaus Metal Workshop,
Germany.
Phyllis B. Lambert Fund. 186.58.

38 ARMCHAIR. 1924. Oak; handwoven wool.
37½" h.
MARCEL BREUER. American, born Hungary 1902.
Manufactured at Bauhaus Carpentry Workshop,
Germany.
Phyllis B. Lambert Fund. 160.58.

THE BAUHAUS

Established successively in Weimar, Dessau and Berlin, from 1919 to 1933 the Bauhaus school was the focal point in the integration of design with the machine age. The school's main workshop at Dessau, designed by Walter Gropius, its founder and first director, was itself one of the great buildings of the 1920s.

Trained simultaneously by artists and master craftsmen, Bauhaus students produced many designs bought and manufactured by industry, which paid royalties to the school. "Bauhaus" became a household word in Germany for the advanced design of the period. The philosophy and teaching methods of Walter Gropius and his distinguished staff are now basic procedures in the training of designers and architects, and "Bauhaus" is still popularly (if often incorrectly) used to describe whatever seems "functional" or "modern."

Bauhaus designers of many nationalities approached problems with a rational simplicity, employing straight lines and using materials with particular inventiveness. They were far more preoccupied with problems of function than were de Stijl artists, but their functional solutions were expressed in geometric forms influenced by Stijl concepts (36). Some Bauhaus ideas that broke with European precedent were the use of metal tubes in the design of furniture and other household objects; stacking furniture designed for easy storage; and highly polished surfaces relieved by textures rather than ornament.

Characteristically geometric Bauhaus objects are the silver teapot by Marianne Brandt (37), the teacup and fruit bowl by Josef Albers (40, 41), and the metal and glass lamp by Jucker and Wagenfeld (39). Writing of this lamp in 1958, Wilhelm Wagenfeld observed that "it was significant for the Bauhaus that its designs were in reality craft products, which through the use of geometrically clear basic shapes gave the appearance of industrial production."

After the rise of Nazism forced the closing of the Bauhaus, many of its members emigrated to the United States. Gropius himself served as chairman of Harvard University's School of Architecture for fifteen years.

39 TABLE LAMP. 1923-24. Glass; chrome-plated metal. 17″ h.
K. J. JUCKER AND W. WAGENFELD. German. Gift of Philip Johnson. 490.53.

ASHTRAYS. 1924. Brass; nickel-plated metal. 2⅝″ h. and 3⅛″ h.
MARIANNE BRANDT. German, born 1893. Gift of John McAndrew. 422.38; 424.38.

JOSEF ALBERS. American, born Germany 1888.

40 TEA GLASS AND SAUCER. 1925. Heat-resistant glass; porcelain; steel; ebony. 2″ h. Gift of Josef Albers. 126.57.

The handles are placed horizontally and vertically to facilitate a change in finger position when serving or accepting a glass of tea. Bauhaus designers were preoccupied with "functional" solutions, especially those that were visually interesting.

41 FRUIT BOWL. 1923. Silver-plated metal; glass; wood. 3⅞″ h., 16⅝″ dia. Gift of Walter Gropius. 190.58.

Manufactured at Bauhaus Metal Workshop, Germany.

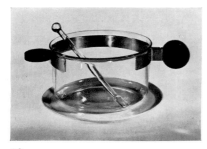

40

41

42 TAPESTRY. 1924. Hand-woven black and white wool; silk; cotton; metal thread. 71″ x 44″. GUNTA SHARON-STÖLZL. Swiss. Phyllis B. Lambert Fund. 75.58.

BAUHAUS TEXTILES. 1923-1928. Wool; cotton; silk; synthetics.

43 ANNI ALBERS. American, born Germany; and
44 GUNTA SHARON-STÖLZL. Swiss. Gift of Anni Albers. 410.51; Phyllis B. Lambert Fund. 76.58.

Bauhaus textile designs developed at the Weaving Workshop were bought by the German textile industry and marketed under the trade name BAUHAUS STOFFE. Stressing the architectural character of fabrics as used in modern buildings, their geometric patterns and textural effects have widely influenced modern textile design.

43
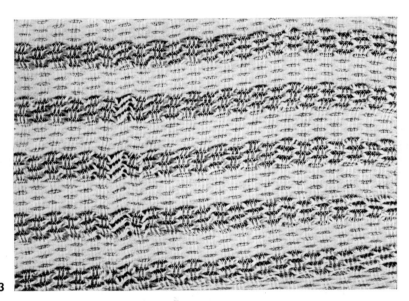

44

45 CEILING FIXTURE. c.1925. Glass; chrome-plated metal. 10½″ h., glass disk 23¾″ dia.
WALTER GROPIUS. American, born Germany 1883.
Mfr.: Bauhaus Metal Workshop, Germany.
Gift of Walter Gropius. 192.58.

46 CHESS SET. 1924. Wood, natural and stained black. 1¾″ h. and ¾″ h.
JOSEF HARTWIG. German. 1880-1954 (?).
Mfr.: Bauhaus Carpentry Workshop, Germany.
Gift of Alfred H. Barr, Jr. 497.58.

45

46

MARCEL BREUER. American, born Hungary 1902.

Mfr.: Gebrüder Thonet A. G., Germany.

47 ARMCHAIR. 1925. Chrome-plated steel tube; canvas. 28″ h.
Gift of Herbert Bayer. 229.34.

48 SIDE CHAIR. 1928. Chrome-plated steel tube; wood; cane. 32″ h.
Purchase. 835.42.

This version of the cantilevered tubular steel chair is the prototype of thousands of variations seen throughout the world.

47

48

49   **50**

Ludwig Mies van der Rohe succeeded Walter Gropius as director of the Bauhaus. Like Mies' highly disciplined architecture, his furniture achieves a classic serenity of line and an unparalleled elegance. He designed the famous Barcelona chair for his German Pavilion at the Barcelona Exposition of 1929. Generally regarded as the classic "monumental" chair of the twentieth century, its imposing scale is due in part to details such as the intersections of its curved legs and the proportions of its tufted leather cushions (49). The cantilevered steel chair (52) is perhaps the simplest and purest statement of this design theme; the armchair version (51) may be compared to the Thonet rocker illustrated on page 11. Like all of Mies' furniture, these designs require impeccable hand-craftsmanship in order to produce, paradoxically, a machine-made appearance.

LUDWIG MIES VAN DER ROHE. American, born Germany 1886.

49 LOUNGE CHAIR (Barcelona chair). 1929. Chrome-plated steel bars; leather. 29½" h.
Mfr.: Knoll Associates, Inc., U.S.A.
Gift of the manufacturer. 552.53.

Designed for the German Pavilion at the 1929 International Exposition, Barcelona.

50 ARMCHAIR (Brno chair). 1930. Chrome-plated steel bars. 32" h.
Gift of Edward M. M. Warburg. 445.56.

Part of the furnishings of the Tugendhat House, Brno, Czechoslovakia, designed by Mies van der Rohe in 1930.

51

52

LUDWIG MIES VAN DER ROHE. American, born Germany 1886.

51 ARMCHAIR. 1926. Chrome-plated steel tube; leather. 32″ h.
Gift of Edgar Kaufmann, Jr. 20.49.

52 SIDE CHAIR. 1926. Chrome-plated steel tube; cane. 30¾″ h.
Anonymous gift. 99.43.
Mfr.: Gebrüder Thonet A. G., Germany.

53

54

During the 1920s design was influenced by movements in the arts besides those having their origin in Holland and Germany. French cubism, for example, contributed forms more varied than those derived from de Stijl.

The furniture designed by the great French architect Le Corbusier, like his painting, sculpture and buildings, reveals a mastery of plastic form and calculated proportion. His reclining chair (55) with a seat frame which can be adjusted to any angle recalls one of his characteristic architectural devices: the lifting of the main part of a building off the ground by columns of distinctly sculptural character. The revolving leather armchair (54) is an adaptation of the swivel chairs used in offices. It also is related to the famous Thonet bentwood armchair (page 10) which Le Corbusier used in his buildings.

LE CORBUSIER (CHARLES-EDOUARD JEANNE-RET). French, born Switzerland 1888. In collaboration with PIERRE JEANNERET AND CHARLOTTE PERRIAND.

53 ARMCHAIR with adjustable back. 1929. Chrome-plated steel tube; black canvas. 23″ h.

54 REVOLVING ARMCHAIR. 1927. Chrome-plated steel tube; red leather. 29½″ h.

55 CHAISE LONGUE, adjustable. 1927. Chrome-plated steel tube; oval steel tubes and sheets, painted green and black; grey jersey; black leather. c.26″ h., 59″ l.
Mfr.: Thonet Frères, France.
Gifts of Thonet Industries, Inc., 281.34; 162.58; 223.50.

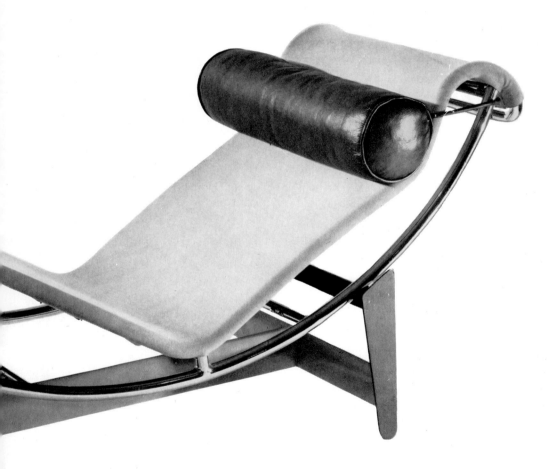

55

MACHINE ART

The precise geometric shapes of seemingly un-designed machines and hand tools became, in the 1920s, a matter of conscious aesthetic preference. Painters, sculptors, architects and even craftsmen were influenced by these pure forms. To describe what thus constitutes the chief design characteristic of our age, the Museum used the phrase "Machine Art" when, in 1934, it exhibited the objects shown on the next three pages.

When making objects in which utility is a secondary consideration, the craftsman is usually free to choose between geometric and non-geometric shapes. Western culture has traditionally held geometric shapes to have a superior beauty, because they call into play the rational mind. Plato, in *Philebus*, de-clared: "I do not mean by beauty of form that of animals or pictures, but . . . straight lines and circles, and the plane or solid figures which are formed out of them by turning-lathes, rulers and compasses; for these I affirm to be not only relatively beautiful, like other things, but they are eternally and abso-lutely beautiful."

In his *Summa Theologica,* St. Thomas Aquinas wrote: "For beauty three things are required. First, then, integrity or perfection: those things which are broken are bad for this very reason. And also a due proportion and harmony. And again clarity: whence those things which have a shining color are called beautiful."

Laboratory glass, as well as propellers (56, 59), coil springs and ball bearings (57) — all of whose shapes are dictated by their function — are beautiful in Plato's sense of the word, and it is a beauty to which the twentieth cen-tury is particularly responsive. Even objects less severely functional, like Walter Dorwin Teague's vase (58) and Frederick Carder's ashtray (60) are conceived and executed with the rigorous precision that characterizes lab-oratory equipment.

56   **57**

56   PROPELLER BLADE. c.1943."Panelyte" (plas-tic and paper). 62¼" h.
Mfr.: St. Regis Paper Co., U.S.A. Company de-sign. Gift of the manufacturer. 243.44.

57   SELF-ALIGNING BALL BEARING. Before 1934. Chrome-plated steel. 8½" dia.
Mfr.: SKF Industries, Inc., U.S.A. Company design. Gift of the manufacturer. 211.34.

59

8

60

61

58 (left to right)
TUMBLERS. Before 1934. Clear crystal. 3⅜″ h.
and 7¾″ h.
WALTER DORWIN TEAGUE. American.
Mfr.: Corning Glass Works—Steuben Division,
U.S.A.
Gift of the manufacturer. 266.34.
BOILING FLASK. Before 1934. Glass. 15″ h.
Mfr.: Corning Glass Works, U.S.A.
Gift of the manufacturer. 224.34.
MEASURING FLASK. Before 1934. Glass.
6¾″ h.
Mfr'd. in Germany for Eimer & Amend.
Gift of Eimer & Amend. 223.34.
SAMPLE OIL BOTTLE. Before 1934. Glass.
6¼″ h.
Mfr.: Owens-Illinois Glass Co., U.S.A.
Gift of the manufacturer. 248.34.

59 BOAT PROPELLER. Before 1934. Brass. 24″
dia.
Mfr.: Sullivan Shipyards, Inc., U.S.A. Company design.
Gift of the manufacturer. S.285.34.

60 ASHTRAY. Before 1934. Clear crystal. 5¼″ sq.
FREDERICK C. CARDER. American, born 1864.
Mfr.: Corning Glass Works—Steuben Division,
U.S.A.
Gift of the manufacturer. 218.34.

61 LABORATORY WARE. Before 1934. Porcelain.
Mfr.: Coors Porcelain Co., U.S.A.
Purchases. 225.34; 251.44.1-2.

CHAIRS

Modern architecture has changed our ideas about furniture by emphasizing a closer relation between indoors and outdoors and advocating a freer use of interior space. Massive storage cabinets are now often built into the walls themselves or are simple rectangles obviously related to the architecture of the room, like windows and hardware. With storage elements thus simplified and often absorbed by architecture, the chair has offered twentieth century furniture designers their most interesting problem. For this reason the Museum's furniture collection, although it includes storage cabinets, desks and tables, is concerned primarily with the development of the chair.

There are two basic solutions to the difficult problem of chair design. The first is the traditional method of shaping individual pieces and then joining them in various ways. Even the revolutionary cantilevered metal chairs by Ludwig Mies van der Rohe (52) and Marcel Breuer (48) fall within this category. Alvar Aalto extended this approach through another technique: a single sheet of plywood is bent in sweeping curves to form a continuous seat and back, suspended within a bent plywood frame (63). The curves make use of the natural springiness of plywood, and the design is an important technical advance.

Russel Wright's wood armchair elaborates the tradition of carved furniture with remarkable forcefulness (67). It anticipated the renewal of interest in sculptural detail seen in much Scandinavian design. Of such work, Hans Wegner's dining chair is the most refined and structurally convincing (68).

The second basic solution to chair design is the direct outgrowth of new techniques and materials, which make it possible to form plywood or plastic into a seat in much the same way that an automobile body is stamped out by a die press. In this way seat, back, and arms can be made in one piece. This technique was employed by Charles Eames and Eero Saarinen for a chair submitted to a furniture competition sponsored by the Museum in 1940. Since then molded plywood and plastic chairs (76, 77) have joined the now classic cantilevered chair as one of the major innovations of twentieth century design.

Chairs made of molded parts usually have been set on more or less conventional supports, producing a maximum contrast with the molded shell (73, 77). However, the technique of molding or stamping material into a complicated shape seems to call for a more truly unified design, whereby the seat and its support appear to be of one and the same material. Eero Saarinen's recent design is a successful example (78). But no one has yet produced a chair that is made *entirely* of one piece of folded or pressed material.

ALVAR AALTO. Finnish, born 1898.

62 SOFA-BED, adjustable. 1930. Chrome-plated steel tube; wool. 24½" h., 80" w.
Mfr.: Wohnbedarf, A. G., Switzerland.
Phyllis B. Lambert Fund. 145.58.

63 LOUNGE CHAIR. c.1934. Molded and bent birch plywood. 25½" h.
Mfr.: Artek OY, Finland.
Gift of Edgar Kaufmann, Jr. 710.43.

62

63

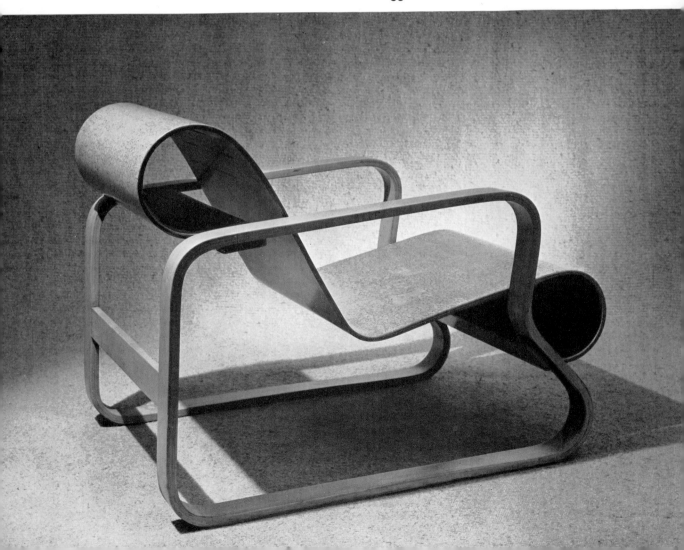

ALVAR AALTO. Finnish, born 1898.
Mfr.: Artek OY, Finland.

64 STOOL. 1954. Laminated ash plywood; leather.
18½″ h.
Phyllis B. Lambert Fund. 147.58.

STOOL. c.1933. Laminated birch plywood. 17¼″ h.
Phyllis B. Lambert Fund. 146.58.

COFFEE TABLE. 1947. Laminated birch plywood;
plate glass. 17½″ h., 29″ sq.
Gift of Edgar Kaufmann, Jr. 19.49.

→

Next two pages

67 ARMCHAIR with adjustable back. 1932. Mahogany; leather; pony skin. 31¼″ h. RUSSEL WRIGHT. American, born 1904. Mfr.: custom-made, U.S.A. Purchase. 150.58.

68 ARMCHAIR. 1949. Oak; cane. 30″ h. HANS WEGNER. Danish, born 1914. Mfr.: Johannes Hansen, Denmark. Gift of Georg Jensen, Inc. 486.53.

65

66

65 ARMCHAIR. 1940. Laminated bent birch plywood; fiber webbing. 34½″ h. BRUNO MATHSSON. Swedish, born 1907. Mfr.: Firma Karl Mathsson, Sweden. Edgar Kaufmann, Jr. Fund. 33.49.

66 RECLINING CHAIR. 1935. Laminated bent birch plywood; upholstered pad. 31½″ h., 53″ d. MARCEL BREUER. American, born Hungary 1902. Mfr.: Isokon Furniture Co., England. Purchase. 836.42.

69 LOUNGE CHAIR. 1938. Metal rod; leather. 35″ h.
ANTONIO BONET; JUAN KURCHAN; JORGE FERRARI-HARDOY. Argentinian.
Mfr.: Artek-Pascoe, Inc., U.S.A.
Edgar Kaufmann, Jr. Fund. 715.43.

70 BEACH SEATS. 1953. Metal tube; canvas. 21″ h.
BILLIE NEWMARCH, American. (designer and manufacturer).
Gift of the manufacturer. 152.58.

71 SIDE CHAIR. 1952. Chrome-plated and black enameled steel; leather. 31¾″ h.
WILLIAM KATAVOLOS; ROSS LITTELL; DOUGLAS KELLEY. American.
Mfr.: Laverne Inc., U.S.A.
Gift of the manufacturer. 151.58.

69 70

71

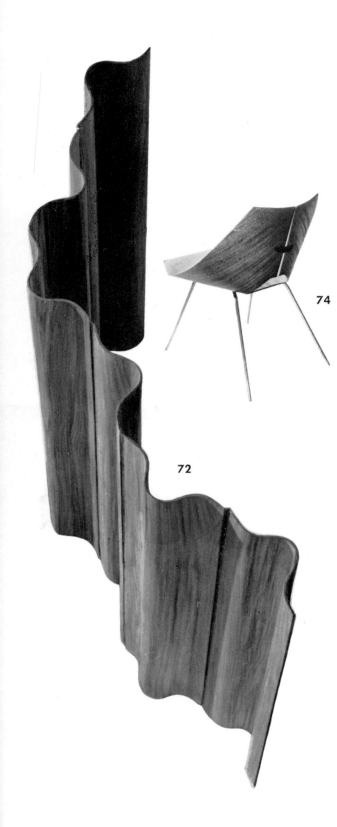

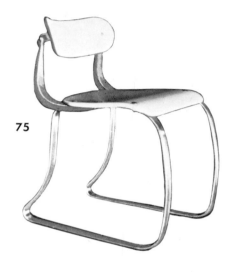

74

75

72

CHARLES EAMES. American, born 1907.

72 FOLDING SCREEN. 1946. Molded ash plywood. 68″ h., c.60″ l.
Mfr.: Evans Products Co., U.S.A.

73 DINING CHAIR. 1946. Molded walnut plywood; metal rod. 29½″ h.
Mfr.: Herman Miller Furniture Co., U.S.A.
Gifts of Herman Miller Furniture Co. 79.48; 553.53.

74 SIDE CHAIR. 1949. Molded walnut plywood; metal rod. 29½″ h.
RAY KOMAI. American, born 1918.
Mfr.: J. G. Furniture Co., U.S.A.
Gift of the manufacturer. 467.51.

75 WORK CHAIR. 1938. Steel; lacquered plywood. 26½″ h.
HERMAN A. SPERLICH. American.
Mfr.: Ironrite Inc., U.S.A.
Gift of the manufacturer. 1659.40.
Designed for use with an ironing machine.

76

76 ARMCHAIR. 1951. Molded plastic reinforced with Fiberglas; wire, enameled black. 31″ h. CHARLES EAMES. American, born 1907. Mfr.: Herman Miller Furniture Co., U.S.A. Gift of the manufacturer. 267.58.

EERO SAARINEN. American, born Finland 1910.

77 LOUNGE CHAIR. 1948. Molded plastic; metal rod; foam rubber. 36½″ h.

78 ARMCHAIR. 1957. Molded plastic reinforced with Fiberglas; aluminum, painted white. 32″ h. Mfr.: Knoll Associates, Inc., U.S.A.

Gifts of the manufacturer. 447.56; 149.58.

77

78

79 COMBINATION DESK-DINING TABLE.
1955-57. Chrome-plated steel; black plastic. Red
enameled metal cabinet. 28″ h., 63″ l.
HANS EICHENBERGER. (Table); Benedikt Rohner
(cabinet). Swiss.
Mfr.: Haussmann & Haussmann, Switzerland.
Phyllis B. Lambert Fund. 154.58.
Roller supports of cabinet allow easy removal
when table is used for dining.

80

CHARLES EAMES. American, born 1907.

80 LOUNGE CHAIR. 1958. Anodized aluminum; Naugahyde. 35¼" h.

81 SOFA. 1954. Chrome-plated steel; foam rubber. 34" h., 71½" w.
Mfr.: Herman Miller Furniture Co., U.S.A.
Gifts of the manufacturer. 148.58; 450.56.

82 ARMCHAIR. 1952. Chrome-plated steel wire. 29¾" h.
Mfr.: Knoll Associates, Inc., U.S.A.
HARRY BERTOIA. American, born Italy 1915.
Mfr.: Knoll Associates, Inc., U.S.A.
Gift of the manufacturer. 268.58.

81

82

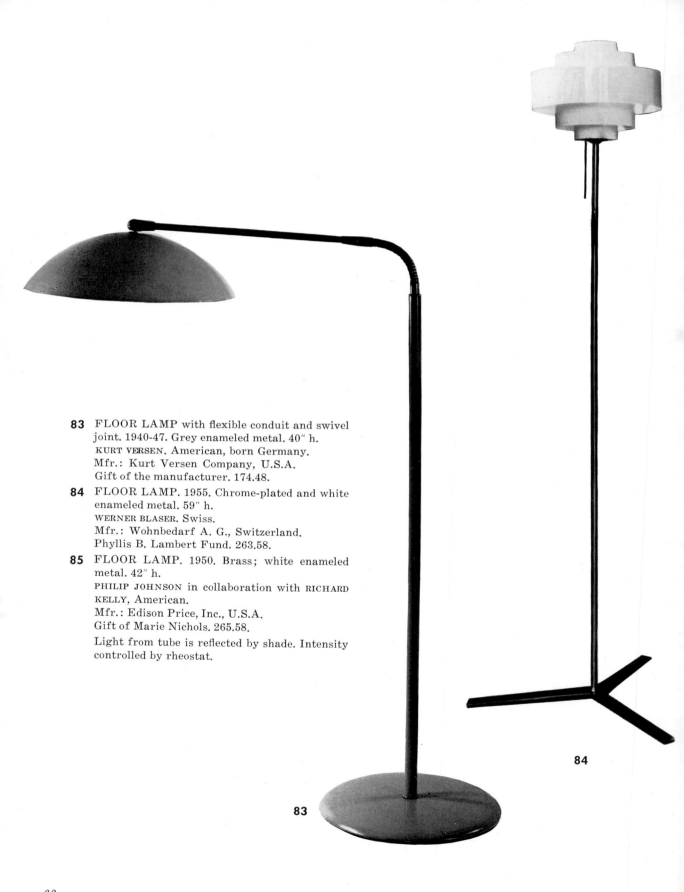

83 FLOOR LAMP with flexible conduit and swivel
joint. 1940-47. Grey enameled metal. 40″ h.
KURT VERSEN. American, born Germany.
Mfr.: Kurt Versen Company, U.S.A.
Gift of the manufacturer. 174.48.

84 FLOOR LAMP. 1955. Chrome-plated and white
enameled metal. 59″ h.
WERNER BLASER. Swiss.
Mfr.: Wohnbedarf A. G., Switzerland.
Phyllis B. Lambert Fund. 263.58.

85 FLOOR LAMP. 1950. Brass; white enameled
metal. 42″ h.
PHILIP JOHNSON in collaboration with RICHARD
KELLY, American.
Mfr.: Edison Price, Inc., U.S.A.
Gift of Marie Nichols. 265.58.

Light from tube is reflected by shade. Intensity
controlled by rheostat.

83

84

LIGHTING

The techniques of lighting within an architectural framework have been highly developed, but the well-designed individual lighting fixture remains a relatively rare object. Too often its main purpose, which is to provide light, is confused with its decorative aspects. These lamps solve a variety of lighting problems, and their decorative qualities derive from the crisp, tool-like finish of their mechanical details.

86

87

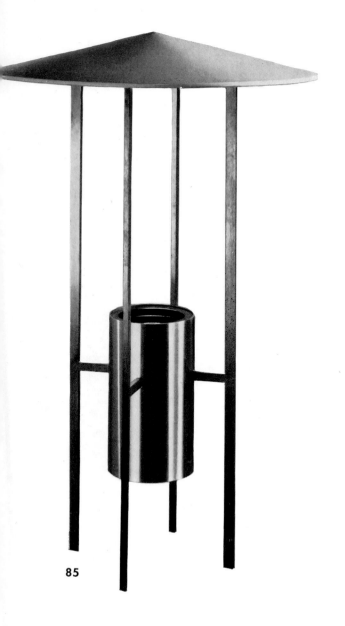

85

86 DESK LAMP with swing arm. 1935. Chrome-plated metal. 16½" h.
WALTER VON NESSEN. American, born Germany. 1889-1943.
Mfr.: Nessen Studio Inc., U.S.A.
Gift of the manufacturer. 453.56.

87 TABLE LAMP. 1957. Clear and translucent plastic. 15¾" h.
YKI NUMMI. Finnish.
Mfr.: Stockmann Orno OY, Finland.
Phyllis B. Lambert Fund. 262.58.

INDUSTRIAL DESIGN

In the early 1900s small appliances for home and office use tended to reveal their mechanical complexity. Sewing machines, for example, would display most of their moving parts and attachments, each piece being articulated as a distinct shape.

As mechanical appliances have become more complex, and as the difficulties of moving, storing and repairing them multiply, an important functional problem the designer must solve is how to protect them. What we see today of most of our mechanical appliances is a shell or package protecting and concealing the machinery within, and many of the objects on the next six pages are simply packages without labels. The Braun radios, however, do make use of printed information, and are indeed superb examples of clearly organized graphic design (92).

But while refrigerators, vacuum cleaners, toasters, sewing machines, and radios have all begun to resemble each other, they have not become beautifully designed anonymous containers. Instead they have arbitrarily borrowed the contours of airplanes or the inflated balloon shapes of the American automobile (until the rise of the tail fin).

Many industrial designers, however, have successfully avoided arbitrary shapes while at the same time selecting from a given object certain functions that may be visually emphasized. The Olivetti office typewriter, perhaps the best design of its kind, and the Necchi sewing machine are sculptural shells distinguished by delicate relationships of curved and flat planes. Together with individually articulated parts, these modulations help suggest how the object performs and how it is to be used (90, 91). The sewing machine in particular benefits from the example of much modern sculpture.

88 ELECTRIC WALL PLUGS. 1956. Hard rubber.
MAX BILL. Swiss.
Mfr.: S.A. des Cableries et Trefileries Cossonay, Switzerland.
Phyllis B. Lambert Fund. 209.58.

89 VACUUM CLEANER. 1956. Red plastic housing. 14½" h.
ACHILLE and PIER GIACOMO CASTIGLIONI. Italian.
Mfr.: R. E. M. di Rossetti Enrico, Italy.
Gift of the manufacturer. SC 6.58.

VACUUM BRUSH. 1955. Blue plastic housing. 5¼" dia.
GIUSEPPE DE GOETZEN. Italian.
Mfr.: Fratelli Chiminello, Italy.
Gift of Philip Johnson. 460.56.

Used for cleaning upholstered furniture.

88   89

90 ELECTRIC SEWING MACHINE. 1956. Metal
housing, enameled ivory and black. 11½″ h.,
18½″ l.
MARCELLO NIZZOLI. Italian.
Mfr.: Vittorio Necchi, S.p.A., Italy.
Gift of the manufacturer. 202.58.

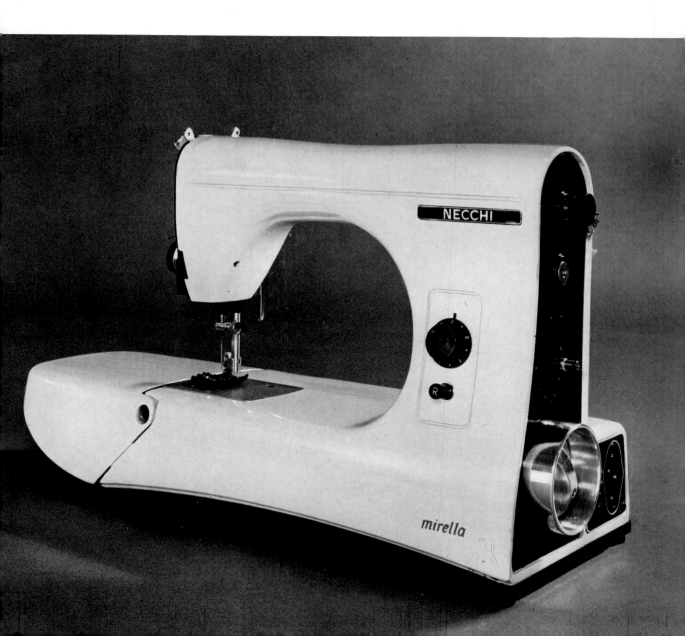

91 OFFICE TYPEWRITER. 1947. Metal housing,
enameled grey. 8½″ h., 13″ w.
MARCELLO NIZZOLI. Italian.
Mfr.: Ing. C. Olivetti e C., S.p.A., Italy.
Gift of Olivetti Corp. of America. 226.50.

Lautstärke

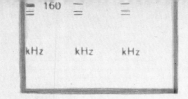

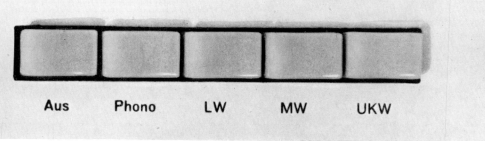

Aus   Phono   LW   MW   UKW

Sender

93

92

94

95

92 RADIO-RECORD-PLAYER. 1956. White plastic and wood housing; clear plastic lid. 9½" h.,
23" w.
DIETER RAMS, German, and HANS GUGELOT, Swiss.

93 DETAIL OF 92.

94 PORTABLE TRANSISTOR RADIO. 1956. Grey
plastic housing; leather strap. 8" h., 11" w.
DESIGN DEPARTMENT BRAUN and DIETER RAMS.
German.
Mfr.: Max Braun, Germany.
Gifts of the manufacturer. 205.58; 206.58.

95 ELECTRIC FAN. 1954. Metal; rubber blades.
Blades 3" l.
EZIO PIRALI. Italian.
Mfr.: Fabbriche Elettrotecniche Riunite, S.p.A.,
Italy.
Gift of Philip Johnson. 459.56.

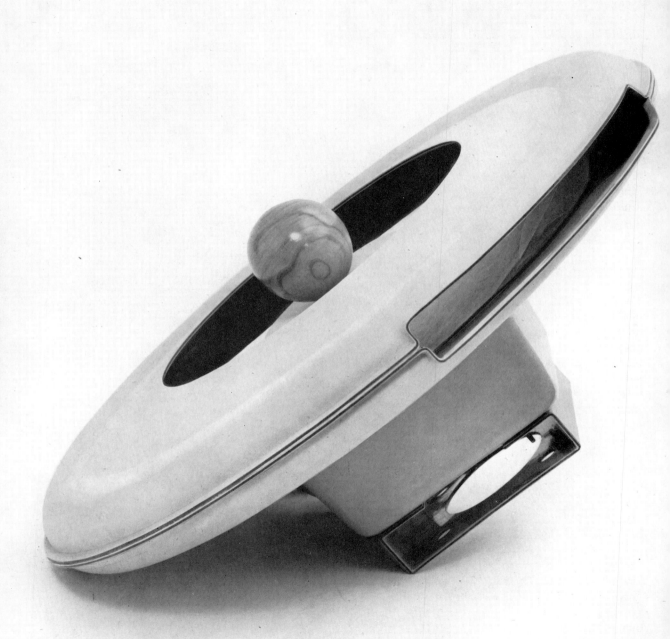

USEFUL OBJECTS: KITCHENWARE

The geometric Machine Art style tended to impose pure forms on all manner of objects as absolute, eternally valid design solutions. But there is no single "answer" to aesthetic "problems," and in the 1930s Machine Art began to evolve toward a freer use of compound curves and sculptural shapes. In their most recent Scandinavian and Italian manifestations these shapes sometimes call to mind the earlier organic forms of Art Nouveau, but they seldom depart completely from the basic discipline of geometry. The objects on the next 14 pages, most of them designed after 1930, range from unadorned geometric forms to equally unadorned but expressively animated shapes, decorative in themselves.

Kitchen equipment is pre-eminently practical, but the variety of practical solutions to the same problem suggests that quite often the designer is decisively influenced by aesthetic preferences. The Trace and Warner teakettle, for example, meets functional requirements with a shape curiously like that of a steel helmet (100). The wire stand for displaying oranges, on the other hand, is an entertaining essay in geometry (99).

In America the enterprising individual who retains complete control of his work by inventing, designing, and sometimes manufacturing and distributing, his own product is not yet a figure of the past. Two such men are Dr. Peter Schlumbohm, a chemist, and Earl C. Tupper. Dr. Schlumbohm brings to the problems of making coffee and boiling water solutions adapted from the chemist's laboratory: his coffeepot and boiling flask (97, 98) are vigorously detailed designs. His electric fan, which uses whirling sheets of filter paper, derives its novel shape from a technical innovation (96). Earl Tupper's numerous plastic containers (104) are distinguished by ingenious hinges, handles and stoppers, and the carefully considered shapes of all these parts are marvelously free of that vulgarity which characterizes so much household equipment.

PETER SCHLUMBOHM. American, born Germany.
Mfr.: Chemex Corporation, U.S.A.

96 ELECTRIC FAN. 1957. Grey plastic and rubber composite housing. 22" dia.
Gift of the manufacturer. 203.58.

97 COFFEE MAKER. 1941. Pyrex glass; wood. 9" h.
Gift of Lewis & Conger. 51.43.

97

98 WATER KETTLE. 1949. Pyrex glass; cork. 11″ h.
PETER SCHLUMBOHM. American, born Germany.
Mfr.: Chemex Corporation, U.S.A.
Gift of the manufacturer. 493.56.

Steam escaping through the cork-tipped glass tube keeps handle cool.

99 DISPLAY STAND FOR ORANGES. c.1946. Metal wire. 11½″ h.
Mfr.: Unknown, U.S.A.
Edgar Kaufmann, Jr. Fund. 210.48.

Used on luncheonette counters.

100 WATER KETTLE. 1939. Cast aluminum. 4¾″ h.
TRACE AND WARNER. American.
Mfr.: Club Aluminum Products Company, U.S.A.
Gift of the manufacturer. 228.44.

101 HOTEL COOKING POTS. 1954. Stainless steel; copper bottoms. 6¾″ h. and 2¼″ h.
W. ARCHIBALD WELDEN. American.
Mfr.: Revere Copper & Brass, Inc., U.S.A.
Gift of the manufacturer. 497.56.

102 COOKING POT. 1955. Stainless steel. 6½″ h.
MASSIMO and ADRIANO LAGOSTINA. Italian.
Mfr.: Emilio Lagostina S.p.A., Italy.
Phyllis B. Lambert Fund. 211.58.

103 MULTIPLE COOKIE CUTTER. c.1940. Tin. 3¼″ h. Mfr.: Unknown, U.S.A.
Purchase. S.380.42.

100

101

102

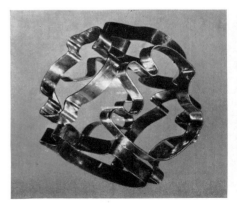

103

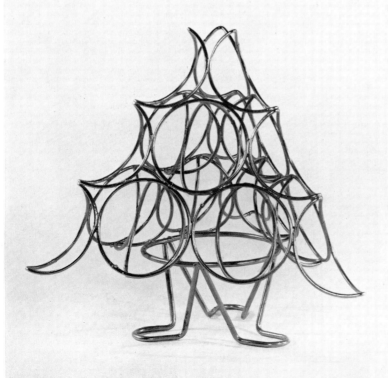

99

104

105

104 KITCHEN CONTAINERS & IMPLEMENTS.
1945-56. Translucent flexible plastic.
EARL S. TUPPER. American.
Mfr.: Tupper Corporation, U.S.A.
Gifts of the manufacturer.

105 COVERED KITCHEN PAIL. 1954. Translucent blue flexible plastic. 10½″ h.
GINO COLOMBINI. Italian.
Mfr.: Kartell-Samco, Italy.
Gift of Philip Johnson. 514.56.

106 STORAGE CONTAINERS with recessed lids for stacking. c.1954. Clear plastic. 1½″ h.
Mfr.: Tri-State Molding Company, U.S.A.
Purchase. 534.56.

KNITTING-WOOL CONTAINER. 1949. Clear and opaque plastic. 9¾″ h.
ELIZABETH MCLENNAN. Canadian.
Mfr.: Toronto Plastic Company, Canada.
Gift of the manufacturer. 515.56.

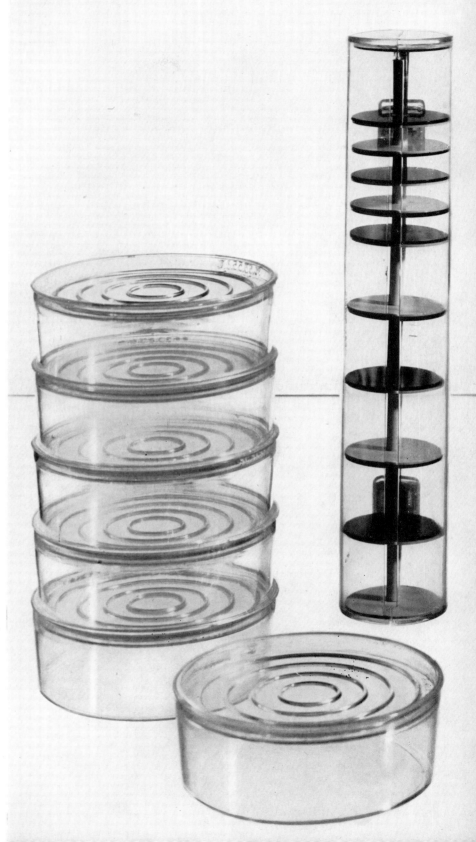

106

USEFUL OBJECTS: TABLEWARE

Some of the precepts that have guided the development of modern furniture and mechanical appliances are also evident in table implements. Like laboratory glass (page 50) most modern tableware depends for its effect on precise geometric shapes whose finely finished surfaces are their sole decoration (108; 109; 112; 113).

A characteristically difficult problem in the design of small objects is the relation of a cup to its handle. A "perfect" teacup is that designed by Trude Petri-Raben in 1929 for Royal Berlin (107). The delicacy of the bowl is complemented by the handle, the shape of which is easy to grasp but is primarily determined by that of the bowl. The entire service is the prototype of modern white porcelain dinnerware.

107 TEACUP and SAUCER. 1927-1933. Porcelain. 1¾" h.
TRUDE PETRI-RABEN. American, born Germany.
Mfr.: Königliche Berliner Porzellanmanufaktur, Germany.
Gift of Fraser's, Inc. 139.52.

108 TUMBLER. 1939-1941. Clear crystal. 5" h.
ELIS BERGH. Swedish.
Mfr.: AB Kosta Glasbruk, Sweden.
Gift of D. Stanley Corcoran. 54.48.

109 TUMBLER. c.1953. Grey crystal. 4" h.
KAJ FRANCK. Finnish.
Mfr.: Wärtsilä-koncernen AB, Finland.
Gift of Wärtsilä Corp., New York. 262.54.

110 TUMBLER. 1953-1954. Multi-colored glass. 5⅞" h.
PAOLO VENINI. Italian.
Mfr.: Venini S.A., Italy.
Gift of Altamira. 468.56.

107

108

109

110

Knives, forks and spoons reflect changing manners as much as changing concepts of design, but the shapes evolved by eighteenth century English silversmiths are still unsurpassed in elegance and refinement. They are the models for such finely balanced silver as that designed by Dominioni and Castiglioni (111). Stainless steel, because it is non-corrosive, may be used for both blade and handle. This technical detail, together with a new evaluation of eating habits, led to Don Wallance's stainless steel flatware in which the knife is a single length of metal curved and twisted to fit the hand (111). The fork, often used as a scoop, ends in short tines.

112

111 FLATWARE: *(Top: left to right)*
1) Stainless steel. 1957.
BERTEL GARDBERG. Finnish.
Mfr.: Fiskars OY, Finland.
Phyllis B. Lambert Fund. SC 12.58.

2) Stainless steel. 1956.
DON WALLANCE. American.
Mfr.: produced in Germany for H. E. Lauffer Co.
Gift of H. E. Lauffer Co. 240.58.

3) Stainless steel. c.1929.
Mfr.: Gottlieb Hammesfahr, Germany.
Gift of Marshall Field. 499.53.

(Bottom: left to right)
1) Hand-wrought silver. 1938.
L. CACCIA DOMINIONI & P. C. CASTIGLIONI. Italian.
Mfr.: Azucena S.R.L., Italy.
Gift of Philip Johnson. 554.53.

2) Stainless steel. 1937.
Mfr.: International Silver Co., U.S.A. Company design.
Purchase. S. 409.38.

112 CREAM PITCHER. 1941-45. Porcelain. 5½″ h.
EVA ZEISEL. American, born Hungary.
Mfr.: Castleton China, Inc., U.S.A.
Gift of the manufacturer. 205.47.

From a formal dinner set developed in collaboration with the Museum of Modern Art.

PITCHER. 1957. Earthenware. 10⅝″ h.
STIG LINDBERG. Swedish.
Mfr.: AB Gustavsberg Fabriker, Sweden.
Gift of the manufacturer. 220.58.

113 ICE BUCKET. 1951. Hand-wrought silver. 4½″ h.
MAGNUS STEPHENSEN. Danish.
Mfr.: Georg Jensen, Ltd., Denmark.
Gift of Philip Johnson. 485.53.

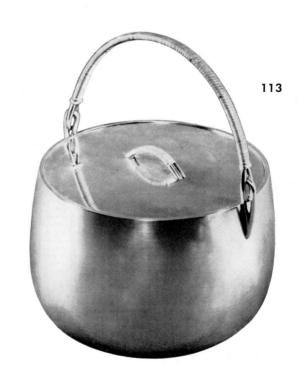

113

114

115

CRAFTS

Although handicrafts are no longer the chief manufacturing source of our common implements, the prototypes for many machine-made objects are first developed by the individual artisan. When not working for industry the craftsman often enriches the characteristic geometric forms of the twentieth century with his particular sensitivity to materials, fulfilling our need for objects which transcend the anonymity of mass production. Excellent examples are the ceramics of Lucie Rie, in which subtle modulations of contour have the highly individual quality of handwriting (115). The Rie ceramics, like those of the Natzlers (116), retain the personalities of their designers while reflecting the widespread influence of Japanese ceramics. Indeed, no other foreign influence has affected twentieth century Western craftsmen as much as the traditional crafts of Japan. The vase by Kitaoji Rosanjin, a Japanese ceramist who has continued his country's tradition and has added refinements of his own, characteristically employs small asymmetrical distortions and planned "accidents" of color and glaze (117).

Glass remains a material of seemingly inexhaustible interest. Its transparency can be made to enhance an architectural idea, as in Alvar Aalto's free-form vase (119). Glass can be made to suggest organic forms, as in Tappio Wirkkala's bowl shaped like a sea anemone (118); and it can even capture the most spontaneous and fleeting images: the Venini vase (120) is a sheet of opaque white glass draped like a handkerchief, but the manner in which the points are pulled up and out suggests microphotographs of drops of liquid at the moment they bounce off a hard surface. Influenced indirectly by technology, the design also recalls the organic forms of Art Nouveau (page 27).

114 TEA SERVICE. 1932. Heat-resistant glass.
WILHELM WAGENFELD. German, born 1900.
Mfr.: Jenaer Glaswerk Schott & Gen., Germany.
Gifts of Philip Johnson and Fraser's, Inc.
222.53; 470-471.56.

115 PITCHER. c.1952. TEAPOT AND CREAMER.
1954. Hand-thrown stoneware with brown and
cream-colored slip glaze. 3½" h; 7" h.; 3¾" h.
LUCIE RIE. English, born Austria. (designer-
craftsman).
Purchase and gift of Bonniers, Inc. 218.54;
461.56.

116

117

116 VASE. c.1943-1946. Hand-thrown pottery with
grey crater glaze. 5½" h.
GERTRUD and OTTO NATZLER. American, born
Austria. (designer-craftsmen).
Gift of Edgar Kaufmann, Jr. 140.48.

117 VASE. 1953. Hand-thrown unglazed red-orange
Bizen ware. 9" h.
KITAOJI ROSANJIN. Japanese. (designer-crafts-
man).
Gift of Japan Society, Inc. 662.54.

118 BOWL. 1953. Translucent crystal. 3½" h.
TAPIO WIRKKALA. Finnish.
Mfr.: Karhula-Iittala, Finland.
Phyllis B. Lambert Fund. 251.58.

119 VASE. 1937. Amber-colored cast glass. 5½" h.
ALVAR AALTO. Finnish, born 1898.
Mfr.: Karhula-Iittala, Finland.
Gift of Artek-Pascoe. 712.43.

Early example of "free form" in a utilitarian object.

120 VASE. 1949. Hand-blown white opaque glass.
c.12½" h.
PAOLO VENINI. Italian.
Mfr.: Venini, Italy.
Gift of Georg Jensen, Inc. 494.53.

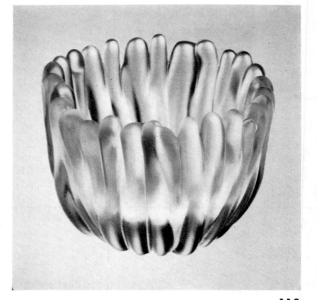

118

119

12

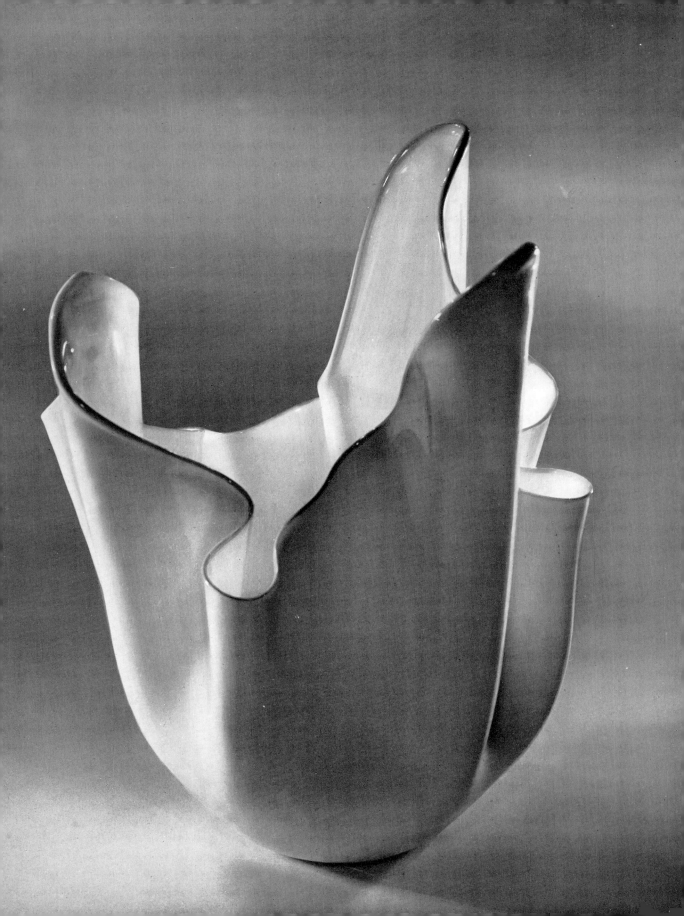

121 ASHTRAY. 1956. Crystal. 1¾″ h.
NANNY STILL. Finnish.
Mfr.: Riihimäen Lasi OY, Finland.
Phyllis B. Lambert Fund. 257.58.

COVERED CONTAINER. 1956. Steel; crystal.
3¼″ h.
SAARA HOPEA. Finnish.
Mfr.: Wärtsilä-koncernen AB, Finland.
Phyllis B. Lambert Fund. 258.58.

122 BOWL. 1951. Hand-ground crystal. 4″ h.
TAPIO WIRKKALA. Finnish.
Mfr.: Karhula-Iittala, Finland.
Purchase. 466.56.

123 BOWL. c.1939. Mexican mahogany. 6″ h.
PLATTER. c.1945. Macassar ebony. 7⅛″ dia.
JAMES PRESTINI. American, born Italy (de-
signer-craftsman).
Edgar Kaufmann, Jr. Fund. 719.43 and
Gift of Dorothy Liebes. 114.57.

124 PLATTER. 1951. Laminated hand-carved ply-
wood. 10½″ l.
TAPIO WIRKKALA. Finnish (designer-craftsman).
Gift of Georg Jensen, Inc. 241.53.

121

122

123

124

126

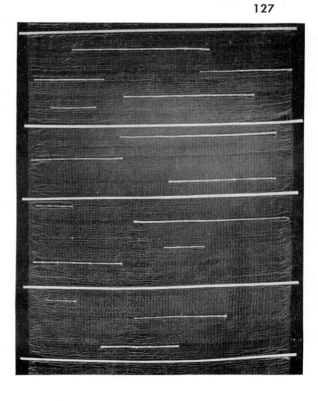

127

Wall hangings of a non-utilitarian nature offer the textile designer unusual opportunities to exploit his materials. Anni Albers' tapestry expressively communicates the mystery of religious feeling through glowing metallic thread (126). Thelma Becherer's transparent wall hanging of plastic thread and dried reeds is an exercise in the purely poetic associations of contrasting materials (127).

125 RUG. 1942. Hand-knotted wool. 6′7″ x 9′.
JOHN FERREN. American. Born 1905.
Mfr.: V'Soske, Inc., U.S.A.
Edgar Kaufmann, Jr. Fund. 718.43.

126 TAPESTRY (LA LUZ II). 1958. Handwoven linen and metal thread. 16½″ x 19½″.
ANNI ALBERS, American, born Germany. (designer-craftsman).
Phyllis B. Lambert Fund. 247.58.

127 TAPESTRY. 1956. Handwoven clear green plastic with dried reeds. 110″ x 34″.
THELMA BECHERER, American. (designer-craftsman). Gift of the artist. 221.57.

VESTMENTS BY MATISSE

"Matisse was eighty years old when he designed the liturgical vestments for the Chapel of the Rosary of the Dominican Nuns at Vence. He was bedridden at the time so that he developed a highly original technique in making the maquettes. He had sheets of paper painted with gouache color which he had mixed himself. With scissors he then cut out the designs and had an assistant pin them up on the ample white walls of his bedroom. Extremely self-critical, he had the elements in the design shifted and repinned again and again; and even then he made two to four maquettes for each of the five different-colored sets of vestments." — A. H. Barr, Jr.

The chasubles are made of silk decorated with appliqué shapes of silk, satin and velvet (128). The shapes suggest by their contours

that they were actually cut with scissors, and the corded outlines used for some of them, as well as the stitching, were also carefully considered as part of the design (129). In color and pattern these vestments bring to liturgical art the spirit of one of the great painters of the twentieth century.

The Museum owns five chasubles: white, red, black, violet, and green; and a stole, maniple, chalice veil and burse.

HENRI MATISSE. French. 1869-1954.

128 CHURCH VESTMENT. c.1950. White silk with yellow satin, green silks and black velvet appliqué. Green and white embroidery stitches. Yellow satin lining. 78½″ w.
Executed by Les Ateliers des Arts Appliqués, Cannes, France. From a set of five vestments. Acquired through the Lillie P. Bliss Bequest, 484.53.

129 DETAIL OF 128.

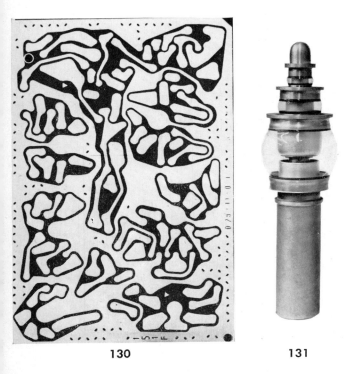

130   **131**

130 PRINTED CIRCUIT. 1958. Plastic sheet; copper foil bonded to surface. 7⅜″ x 5″.
Engineering Dept., Warwick Mfg. Co., E. Hassler, Director. American.
Mfr.: Cronane Inc. for Warwick Mfg. Co., U.S.A.
Gift of the manufacturer. SC 15.58.
Used in television sets.

131 HIGH-POWER TRIODE. 1954. Rhodium plated copper and other metals; heat resistant glass. 15½″ high.
CHARLES V. WEDEN (electrical design); GEORGE AGULE (design). American.
Mfr.: Machlett Laboratories, Inc., U.S.A.
Gift of the manufacturer. SC 14.58.1.
Used in industrial electronic heating.

132 CONTROL PANEL for IBM 305 — Random Access Memory Accounting Machine (RAMAC). 1950. Aluminum frame; aluminum wires covered with colored plastic. 20¾″ x 11¼″.
IBM Product Development Laboratory.
Mfr.: International Business Machines Corp., U.S.A.
Gift of the manufacturer. SC 13.58.

THE NEW MACHINE ART

Most often the design of machines is not consciously guided by aesthetic considerations. But in technology as in science, the more limited aesthetic decisions may be, the more significant are their effects. For this reason Machine Art still offers important clues to emerging concepts of design, the word design being understood not only in its conventional sense but also as a broad approach to the making and organizing of objects.

Since the end of World War II electronics has altered our conception of how things need to be shaped in order to work, and of how they may be related to each other. Geometric machine art (page 48) suggested by its finite shapes the direct action of push and pull: the new machines are incomprehensible unless one knows about the existence of invisible forces. Even the tubes designed and manufactured by Machlett Laboratories do not visually explain themselves, although they are still related to earlier geometric shapes (131).

Perhaps the most striking characteristic of the new machine aesthetic is its dematerialization of finite shapes into diagrammatic relationships. Examples are the printed electrical circuits, which replace separate three-dimensional objects with groups of patterns printed on a flat surface (130). Such patterns can hardly be said to have precise boundaries, or to be complete in themselves. This is also evident in a three-dimensional design such as the control panel from a RAMAC computer, with its clusters of colored wires arranged on a panel according to the requirements of computing operations (132).

Artists and designers are more and more concerned with the philosophical concepts underlying technology. Dematerialization and pattern relationships recall similar ideas in painting, most notably in the work of Jackson Pollock. The practical effect of these ideas on the design of commonplace useful objects is not yet apparent, but we may reasonably expect that they will in time produce a new attitude toward form.

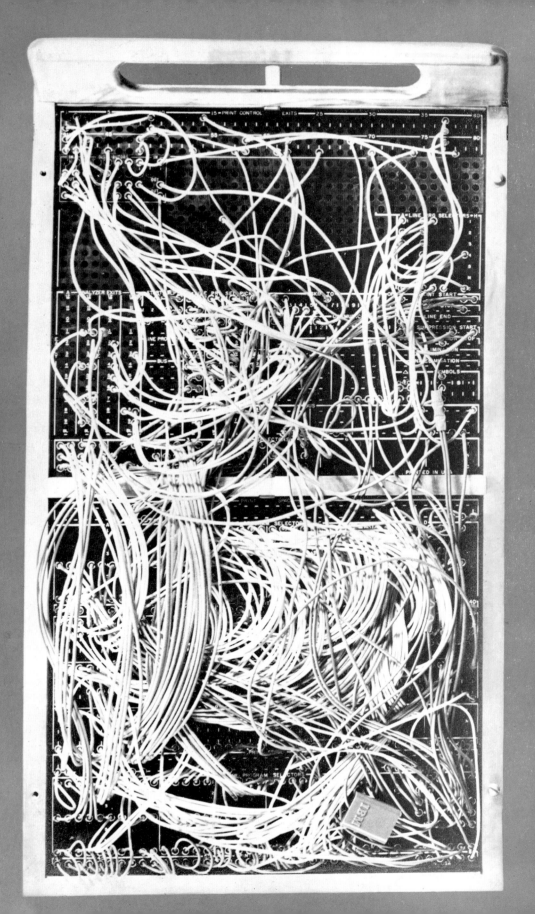

The Design Collection has been photographed by GEORGE BARROWS.

Additional photographs used in this book as follows:

Ralph Baxter, 96
Charles Eames, 72, 80
Foto-studio "Casali," 105
Andreas Feininger at Black Star, 103
Alexandre Georges, 122, 128
Herbert Matter, 78, 82
Aarne Pietinen OY, 124
David Royter, 10, 47, 48, 51, 57, 63, 66, 67
Soichi Sunami, 8, 17, 36, 56, 91, 125, 129, 133
Peter Trüb, 52
Hans Van Nes, 24
photo courtesy Max Braun, Germany, 92